The Common People
Heard Him Gladly

JAMES W. MOORE

The Common People Heard Him Gladly

A LENTEN STUDY FOR ADULTS

Abingdon Press / Nashville

THE COMMON PEOPLE HEARD HIM GLADLY:
A LENTEN STUDY FOR ADULTS

Copyright © 2004 by Abingdon Press.

Scripture quotations, unless otherwise noted, are from the New Revised Standard Version of the Bible, copyright © 1989, by the Division of Christian Education of the National Council of the Churches of Christ in the United States of America. Used by permission.

Scripture quotations noted KJV are from the King James or Authorized Version of the Bible.

Scripture quotations noted RSV are from the Revised Standard Version of the Bible, copyright © 1946, 1952, 1971 by the Division of Christian Education of the National Council of the Churches of Christ in the USA. Used by permission.

This book is printed on acid-free, elemental chlorine–free paper.

ISBN 0-687-063442

04 05 06 07 08 09 10 11 12 13 — 10 9 8 7 6 5 4 3 2 1

MANUFACTURED IN THE UNITED STATES OF AMERICA

For the members of

St. Luke's United Methodist Church

Houston, Texas

Who never cease to amaze me

With their love, loyalty, commitment,

and their

Christlike graciousness

Contents

Introduction:
The Common People
Heard Him Gladly

SCRIPTURE: *Read Mark 12:35-37.*

Can you imagine the excitement that danced in the hearts of the people in Galilee some 2,000 years ago when the word came that Jesus was heading their way? "Jesus is coming!" the cry would go up, and the people would drop what they were doing and rush out with strong anticipation to see him or hear him or touch him. Wherever he went, it was the same. Great crowds would clamor to be near him and to hear him.

In Mark 12:37, we find that fascinating sentence that sums it all up: "And the large crowd was listening to him with delight." The King James Version translates it like this: "And the common people heard Him gladly." Why was this so? What was it about Jesus that attracted the masses to him? Why did he resonate with regular, ordinary folks? Why did they come from far and near just to get a glimpse of him? What was his appeal? What was his authority?

Whatever it was, it was powerful—and, as a matter of fact, it still is. Here is how James Francis expressed it in that classic piece entitled *One Solitary Life*:

> Here is a man who was born in an obscure village, child of a peasant woman. He grew up in another obscure village. He worked in a carpenter shop until He was thirty, and then for three years was an itinerant preacher.
>
> He never wrote a book. He never held an office. He never

owned a home. He never had a family. He never went to college. . . . He never traveled two hundred miles from the place where He was born. He never did one of the things that usually accompany greatness. He had no credentials but himself. . . .

While still a young man the tide of popular opinion turned against Him. His friends ran away. One of them denied Him. Another betrayed Him. He was turned over to His enemies. He went through the mockery of a trial. He was nailed upon the cross between two thieves. His executioners gambled for the only piece of property He had on earth while He was dying, and that was His coat. When He was dead, He was taken down and laid in a borrowed grave through the pity of a friend.

Nineteen wide centuries have come and gone and today He is the center of the human race and the leader of the column of progress.

I am far within the mark when I say that all the armies that ever marched, and all the navies that were ever built, and all the parliaments that ever sat and all the kings that ever reigned, put together, have not affected the life of man upon this earth as powerfully as has this one solitary life.[1]

What was it about Jesus that touched people so deeply and so dramatically? What was it about Jesus that caused people to crowd the Jericho roadsides in hopes of getting even a quick glimpse of him? What was it about Jesus that caused those who were sick and those who had physical disabilities to seek him out? What was it about Jesus that caused an entire city of people to come to the house where he was staying and gather at the door? What was it about Jesus that caused those fishermen at the Sea of Galilee to drop their fishing nets and leave their boats and follow him? Why did persons who were blind call out to him? Why did those who were poor gather around him? Why did the outcasts of society feel wanted and welcomed, loved and accepted, in his presence?

Why did the multitudes gather on the Galilean hillside to hear him speak? What was it about Jesus that caused that woman with internal bleeding to fight her way through the crowd just to touch the hem of his robe? What was it about Jesus that caused parents to bring their children to him? Why did people of diverse backgrounds and different races and varying philosophies feel that he had the key to life and the answer to their problems? What was it about Jesus that caused the common people to hear him gladly?

Well—*many* things. Let me list a few ideas about this for our consideration.

First, the Common People Heard Him Gladly Because He Brought Them Good News

Jesus brought the people the good news of salvation! The Gospel writers saw this vividly, and they recorded it. For example, Luke announced the birth of Jesus as "good news of great joy" (Luke 2:10). Also in Luke's Gospel, look at how Jesus began his ministry. First, he was baptized by John. Next, he went into the wilderness to meditate and to think through his ministry. Then he was ready to begin. But notice what he did first: He went to the synagogue at Nazareth, and he stood up and read this passage from Isaiah as a preface to his ministry:

> The Spirit of the Lord is upon me, / because he has anointed me / to bring good news to the poor. / He has sent me to proclaim release to the captives / and recovery of sight to the blind, / to let the oppressed go free, / to proclaim the year of the Lord's favor.
> (Luke 4:18-19)

Then Jesus put the scroll down and said, in effect, "Today, in your very hearing, this text has come true!" (Luke 4:21). In Matthew's Gospel, John the Baptist sent his disciples to Jesus with a pointed question: "Are you the one who is to come, or are we to wait for another?" (11:3).

What was going on here? Well, remember that Jesus and John were cousins; and Cousin John was being a bit sarcastic. "When are you going to get with the program?" he was essentially asking. "When are you going to bring this kingdom? When are you going to start acting like the Messiah?"

Remember how Jesus answered: "Go and tell John what you hear and see: the blind receive their sight, the lame walk, the lepers are cleansed, the deaf hear, the dead are raised, and the poor have good news brought to them" (Matthew 11:4-5). You see, the fact is that people then as now were starving for some "good news." Religion for many of the people back then had become cold, staid, authoritarian, negative, prohibitive, irrelevant, fearsome, and sometimes even abusive and exploitive. Religion, to them, did not speak to their hurts. It did not bring them joy.

People heard Jesus gladly because he brought them good news. Over and over again, he said to them, "You count! You matter! Fear not! Don't be afraid! God loves you! God is with you!"

Let me make the point with a parable written by the noted preacher Dr. Fred Craddock. One evening a farmer named John was heading for home, and he was running late. He tried to take a shortcut across an unfamiliar field. But he fell into an old, abandoned cistern, a deep, deep hole. He was a proud and strong man, so he said, "I can get out of here." John was knee-deep in mud and sand, however. He reached to the sides of the cistern, mossy green and slick and wet; but he had no leverage. He could not get out. Finally he swallowed his pride and cried out, "Help, help!"

A neighbor walking by heard his cry and looked down in there and said, "John, is that you? I can't believe you are down there! Look at you down there in that ugly hole—an embarrassment to your family, an embarrassment to yourself. You are a disgrace!" The neighbor really told him off. Then the neighbor went on into town and told everybody about it and how he had told John off. The neighbor said, "I've been wanting to say that for years!" It was quite a speech, but John was still in the hole. John continued to cry out for help—more desperately now.

Next, a couple of politicians came by and saw John's plight; and they were upset. They said, "This is awful! This should have been taken care of years ago!" So they went into town; got the city council together; passed a law; and then came out and put up a sign that read, "Twenty-five-dollar fine to fall in this hole." And it was a good law, they said—"It needed to be passed."

John was still in the hole, however. John cried out louder, "Help, help, help!" Some people driving by heard his cries. They looked down into the hole and said, "This is a disgrace to our community. We can't have this." So they notified the beautification committee, and they came out and planted some azaleas and dogwoods and yellow roses. It was beautiful, but John was still down in the hole.

Now, with raspy voice and almost no hope left, John called out, "Please, somebody . . . help me! Help!" Just about then a man came by, and he looked down there and saw John in this awful fix. He had compassion in him; and he said, "Let me help you. I can get you out. Here . . . take 'hold of my hand." And in that moment, the only thing important in John's world was that hand.[2]

Do you know who that was? Do you know whose hand it was that pulled John out of that hole? Of course you do. Most of us recognize that hand, and most of us remember how he pulled us up and out and saved us. That is the good news of our faith, isn't it? Others may scoff at us or fuss at us or ignore us, but Christ wants to get on with the saving!

In the powerful movie *The Hiding Place*, Corrie ten Boom (magnificently portrayed by our dear friend Jeannette Clift George) says this: "There is no pit so deep that God is not deeper still!" That is why the common people heard Jesus gladly: He brought them good news, the good news of salvation.

Second, the Common People Heard Him Gladly Because He Practiced What He Preached

In Mark 12, Jesus talks about hypocrisy, exposing it for what it is:

> Beware of the scribes, who like to walk around in long robes, and to be greeted with respect in the marketplaces, and to have the best seats in the synagogues and places of honor at banquets! They devour widows' houses and for the sake of appearance say long prayers. They will receive the greater condemnation. (verses 38-40)

13

The people heard Jesus gladly because they were fed up with hypocrisy, and they knew he was no hypocrite. He meant what he said. He practiced what he preached. He saw faith as a style of living. He was authentic, genuine; and the people sensed it, felt it, knew it.

A few years ago I was on a preaching mission in another city. One evening during the worship service, a high-school-age girl gave a magnificent devotional talk. She spoke of love as the key sign and symbol of the Christian faith. She encouraged us to be thoughtful, considerate, and kind. She finished her comments with a beautiful paraphrase of 1 Corinthians 13, known as the love chapter. All of us were impressed. The congregation was visibly moved. But after the service I heard this same young girl, who had just spoken so powerfully on the importance of love, talking to her mother in the church parking lot. Her mother had been five minutes late picking her up, and she was upset because she had missed five minutes of a television program. She spoke to her mother in a cruel, vicious tone. She called her mother "stupid," an "old fool," and another profane name that I will not repeat. She was arrogant, haughty, rude, and hostile, the very opposite of what she had proclaimed in the sanctuary only moments before. I felt so sad, so let down, because we want people to practice what they preach.

The common people heard Jesus gladly because he brought them good news, and he practiced what he preached.

Finally, the Common People Heard Jesus Gladly Because to Him, They Were Not Common

To Jesus, the people were *not* common; they were special! Each was unique. Each was valued. Each was a child of God to be loved and respected. Jesus did not see them as second-rate. He did not shun them as outcasts, as though they were beneath him. He did not abuse them or exploit them or look down his nose at them. That is why the common people heard him gladly. To him, they were not common. He made them feel valuable, important, cherished, cared for, accepted, and loved. He met them where they were. He went to them and helped them. He spoke their language. He did not talk down to them from some cold, remote ivory tower. No, he mingled with them, visited with them, listened to them, ate with them, accepted them as persons of integrity and worth; and ultimately he died for them— and for us!

Some years ago, a great baseball player set a new Major League record, an accomplishment that still stands. After he achieved this accomplishment on national television, congratulations poured in to this player from all over the country. Hundreds and hundreds of letters and telegrams came from baseball fans everywhere. One reporter, aware of the warm response, said to him, "You have received all those letters and telegrams. Were any of them special?" I like this baseball player's answer. He said, "They were all special to me!"

That answer had the spirit of Christ written all over it. *All* the people were special to Christ back then; and you know, they still are. *You* are special to him. That person next to you at home, at work, or in church is special to him. To Jesus Christ, there are no common people; there are no second-class citizens; there are no misfits; there are no outcasts. *There are only children of God.*

So this is the good news of the Christian faith. You can have his love! I can have his love! It is given freely, intentionally, enthusiastically, graciously! *All we have to do is accept it.*

If you feel right now like you are down in a hole, in some deep pit, there is a hand reaching out to you, a hand that can pull you up and out, a hand that can save you. If you feel down and out right now, won't you take hold of that hand?

In the pages that follow, we will look at some of the people who heard Jesus gladly and took hold of his hand. We will discover that these people were regular folks, folks like you and me. We will also see that some of them not only heard Jesus gladly, they remained faithful to him for the rest of their lives.

But then, there is Judas. What about him? How does he fit in? Why is he here in the pages of this study? The reason is that he is the dramatic reminder that people can hear Jesus gladly at first and then later "throw in the towel."

So, the real question for you and me is this: How is it with us right now? (This is, after all, the question of the Lenten season.) Ask yourself, *Am I faithful to the call of Christ or not? Will I continue to hear him gladly, or will I fall away? Will I continue to trust him; or will I, too, betray my Master?*

As we go through this study, my hope and prayer is that we all will be inspired by these powerful biblical stories to grow in our discipleship, to become more committed in our faithfulness, and to draw even closer to our Christ.

Study / Discussion Questions

1. List and discuss some of the many messages of good news Jesus brought to people during his ministry.

2. How was Jesus' "religion"—in this sense, his message and his methods—different from the religion of his times? What do people look for today in their religion and in their religious leaders?

3. Give an example of how Jesus practiced what he preached. How was Jesus "real"? What are some qualities of "realness" or authenticity that you admire in others?

4. What can we as Christians today learn from Jesus' treatment of others? How was he an example?

5. Why is it easier to see and find differences in others rather than to see what we have in common? In what ways do we judge others without really knowing them?

6. What was necessary in order to hear Jesus during his ministry? What is necessary for us to hear Jesus' message today?

Prayer

Dear God, thank you for the opportunity to hear your message of love and salvation. Help us to remember your example in Jesus Christ as we encounter others and minister to their needs. May people see your love through our words and deeds. Amen.

Focus for the Week

Look for common bonds this week. Take a close look at the people with whom you come into contact. Think about what you have in common with others. Initiate a conversation with a stranger. Consider how we all are God's children.

Notes

1. From http://www.sjvls.org/sjvis/bens/bf007sl.html
2. From a lecture series presented by Dr. Fred Craddock at First United Methodist Church, Longview, Texas.

Jesus and Andrew: "The Ripple Effect"

SCRIPTURE: *Read John 1:35-42.*

Have you heard that story about the little dog who had been hit by a car and was left wounded by the side of the road? A kindhearted doctor drove by and saw the injured dog. He stopped his car, picked up the dog tenderly, and took him home with him. The doctor carefully examined the dog and found that the little pup had been stunned and had suffered a few cuts and abrasions but was otherwise all right.

With expert hands the doctor revived the dog, cleaned up the wounds, and gave the little dog the tender love and care he so much needed. The doctor decided to prepare a comfortable place out in the garage for his new patient. He wanted to let the little dog spend the night there so that he could check him over in the morning. But as the doctor was carrying the injured animal from the house out to the garage, the dog suddenly jumped from his arms and scampered off. *What an ungrateful little mutt,* the doctor said to himself, with a smile.

The next morning the doctor realized how wrong he was about that, however. There was an urgent scratching at his front door. When he opened it, there was the little dog he had treated. The dog had come back, but this time the dog was not alone. With him was another hurt dog!

That is the story of "The Ripple Effect." Throw a stone into a lake; the water then ripples out, and the circle widens. One of the great characteristics of the first Christians was their ripple effect. Something wonderful had happened to them. Jesus Christ, the Great Physician, had touched their hurt lives and had brought healing and wholeness. These persons were so filled with joy and gladness that they just could not contain it. They had to share it. They could not sit still. It was contagious. It spread out among the people in a ripple effect. And the circle grew wider and wider. It was the "Each One Teach One," "Each One Bring One," "Each One Tell One" method; and it worked.

One of the most beautiful examples of the ripple effect is recorded in the first chapter of John's Gospel, where Andrew finds the Messiah and then quickly runs to share the good news with his brother, Simon. The passage reads, "One of the two who heard John speak and followed him was Andrew, Simon Peter's brother. He first found his brother Simon and said to him, 'We have found the Messiah'" (verses 40-41). Then Andrew brought Simon Peter to Jesus. Like that hurt little puppy who had found help and healing, he ran to get his brother.

In many ways, Andrew was an ordinary man. There is not much in the Scriptures to distinguish him—at least, not in the ways by which we usually measure greatness. So far as we know, Andrew performed no mighty deeds. He preached no great sermons. He did nothing extraordinary that we would classify as outstanding. He just served in his humble way. He just did what needed to be done without fanfare. No complaining, no griping, no questioning, no bellyaching; Andrew was too big for that kind of pettiness. To Andrew, all that mattered was to be with the Lord and to serve him as well as he could.

William Barclay, the noted Bible scholar, wrote some remarkable words about Andrew some years ago. He said this:

> We do not possess a great deal of information about Andrew, but even the little that we do know of him perfectly paints his character. Andrew is one of the most attractive characters in the apostolic band [because] . . . Andrew is characteristically the man who was always introducing others to Jesus. There are only three times in the gospel story when Andrew is brought into the centre of the stage. There is the incident here [in John 1], in which Andrews brings Peter to Jesus. There is the incident in *John 6:8, 9*

when Andrew brought to Jesus the boy with the five loaves and two small fishes. And there is the incident in *John* 12:22 when Andrew brought the enquiring Greeks into the presence of Jesus. It was Andrew's great joy to bring others to Jesus. He stands out as the man whose one desire was to share the glory. He is the man with the missionary heart. Having himself found the friendship of Jesus, he spent all [his] life in introducing others to that friendship. Andrew is our great example in that he could not keep Jesus to himself.[1]

In other words, Andrew is the dramatic symbol of "The Ripple Effect." In him, we see how it works. Let's take a closer look and see what we can learn from him.

First of All, It Is Important to See That Andrew Was Open to New Truth

Andrew lived in a time when it was easy to be close-minded. Indeed, it was dangerous to wonder about or question the established laws and traditions of that day. Being open to new truth could get you into trouble back then.

But along came John the Baptist with some new ideas, and Andrew listened and understood what he was talking about; and Andrew followed him. Andrew was a disciple of John the Baptist, but then along came Jesus. Andrew, always open to new truth, realized immediately that Jesus was extra-special; and he gave up everything to follow him. Andrew's mind was open, and he responded quickly. Put that over against others, who, upon hearing about Jesus, said, "How could anything good come out of Nazareth?" What a great lesson to learn from Andrew, since we constantly are tempted to quit thinking, to stop growing, and to give in to the sin of the closed mind.

Back in the mid-1930s, a young man named Theodor Geisel developed a new style for writing books. His approach was so different, so unusual, that he could not get anybody to take him seriously. People were close-minded about him. He got no encouragement from anybody. But, nevertheless, he persisted. He put his book together and sent it off to a publisher. That publisher rejected it. He sent it to another publisher; and that publisher rejected it, too. Nobody encouraged him at all, but he kept trying.

Twenty-three times it happened. Twenty-three different publishers closed their minds to Theodor Geisel and refused even to consider publishing his book with its unusual new style. But, finally, the twenty-fourth publisher he approached decided to give it a shot and put his book in print. That book sold six million copies! By the way, Theodor Geisel's middle name was Seuss; his pen name was Dr. Seuss!

The point is clear: Close-mindedness can be costly in every arena. It may be especially costly in the arena of faith. This is the first great lesson we learn from Andrew. It is so important to be open to God's new truth. It is so dangerous to give in to the sin of the closed mind. First of all, Andrew was open to new truth.

Second, Andrew Was Eager to Share With His Brother

Don't you just love that about Andrew? When he met Jesus and heard him and sensed how special Jesus was, Andrew could not wait to get home and share the good news with his brother, Simon. He went home and found Simon and brought him back to meet Jesus. Isn't that something? Andrew was too bighearted to hoard this wonderful experience. He had to share it with his brother. Andrew was bighearted, magnanimous, generous, eager to share. Because of his bigness of spirit, great things happened. Andrew knew about love.

Recently someone put a clipping on my desk. It was taken from a magazine, and it touched me. It is entitled "The Mystery of Love," and it reads like this:

> Love makes you feel special. It changes everyone for the better. It is the one commodity that multiplies when you give it away. The more you spread it around, the more you are able to hang on to it. . . . It keeps coming back to you. . . . It cannot be bought or sold. So give it away! . . . Empty your pockets! . . . Shower it on everyone—even those who don't deserve it! You may startle

them into behaving in a way you never dreamed possible. . . . Not only is love the sweet mystery of life, it is also the most powerful motivator known to humankind.

Andrew was a caring person, a loving person who was eager to share with his brother. If only we could learn that lesson from Andrew, life would be better for all of us, wouldn't it? Andrew was open to new truth, and he was eager to share with his brother.

Third, Andrew Was Willing to Do the Little Things

Andrew's dependability in the mundane things and his willingness to do the little detail work, the behind-the-scenes tasks, reminds us that to be responsible in small matters is to have in you the stuff of greatness. Great things do not just happen. Stars are not born overnight. Significant accomplishments come only from a long series of little things done well.

The story is told that when Beethoven was in the middle of his great career, he was surrounded one evening by a group of admirers who were amazed by his piano magic. One woman who was especially enthusiastic said, "Oh, Maestro, if only God had given me that gift of genius!" Beethoven replied, "It is not genius, Madame, nor magic. It's hard work. All you have to do is practice on your piano eight hours a day for forty years, and you'll be as good as I am."

Some years ago, the Queen of England complimented Paderewski, calling him a genius. Paderewski responded, "Before I was a genius, I was a drudge."[2]

In a safari park in the African nation of Kenya, there is a sign that reads, "Visitors who throw litter in the crocodile pit will be asked to retrieve it." Someone asked the park manager if the sign weren't a bit extreme. He replied, "Well, yes, I suppose it is—but it does help people to be more responsible in small matters."

Andrew was responsible in small matters. He could run and get his brother or find a small boy in a crowd or fetch a donkey with the best of them. He could do ordinary things in extraordinary ways. That was the greatness of Andrew. He was responsible, and he was willing to do the little things. Andrew was open to new truth. He was eager to share with his brother. He was willing to do the little things.

Fourth and Finally, Andrew Was Never Jealous or Resentful

How easy it would have been for Andrew to be envious of his brother, Simon. Think about that. How would you feel if you brought your brother into a group and he then quickly zipped in front of you and got so much attention, so many accolades, and got to do so many great things? Would you be jealous or envious or resentful? Andrew was not. It did not seem to bother him at all. He was quite content to stand back and let his brother have the limelight. He was quite content to work in the background in his modest, humble way with no jealousy or bitterness at all. That kind of "bigness" is the spirit of the saints. Frederick Buechner put it like this:

> The love for equals is a human thing—of friend for friend, brother for brother. It is to love what is loving and lovely. The world smiles.
>
> The love for the less fortunate is a beautiful thing—the love for those who suffer. . . .
>
> This is compassion, and it touches the heart of the world.
>
> The love for the more fortunate is a rare thing—to love those who succeed where we fail, to rejoice without envy with those who rejoice. . . . The world is always bewildered by its saints.[3]

Resentment, envy, and jealousy are so dangerous because they can slip up on the best of people. Remember Oscar Wilde's famous story about this. The devil comes upon a group of people who are trying to torment a holy man. They are trying to break his spirit, but to no avail. He resists every temptation with poise and serenity. They tempt him with all sorts of worldly pleasures; but the holy man is steadfast, unbending in his commitment.

Finally, after watching for a while, the devil says to the tempters, "You are going about this all wrong. Your methods are too crude, too obvious. Permit me." Then the devil walks over and whispers into the ear of the holy man, "Have you heard the news? Your brother has just been made the Bishop of Alexandria!" Immediately a malignant scowl of jealousy clouds the formerly serene face of the holy man!

Jealousy: Is that your problem? Is that your weakness? Is that your sin? Andrew shows us how beautiful it is to be open to new truth, to be eager to share with our brothers and sisters, to be willing to do the little things. Andrew shows us the power of "The Ripple Effect."

Study / Discussion Questions

1. List and discuss the qualities Andrew possessed that Christians today should try to emulate. What do you like most about Andrew and his style of ministry?

2. In your own words, explain the meaning of "The Ripple Effect." Share a time when you were part of a ripple effect.

3. What makes it difficult at times to be open to new truth? What has been your biggest stumbling block in this? What are some of the costs of close-mindedness?

4. Discuss the importance of being responsible for the details. Why is this crucial in ministry? Are you a detail-oriented person? Explain how you operate.

5. When you are jealous or resentful, how does it hurt both you and others? How does one obtain "bigness" of spirit?

6. Recall a time when you were eager to share good news with someone. What motivates people to want to share? How does this apply to Christian ministry?

Prayer

Dear God, you started a ripple effect when Jesus came into the world. Help us to carry on his messages of hope, love, peace, and salvation that our world needs so much today.

Thank you for always being with us in the tough times of life. Amen.

Focus for the Week

Remember the ministry of Andrew this week. Think about what made him so effective in ministry. Serve the Lord to the best of your ability. Look for ways to touch people's lives through love and kindness.

Notes

1. From *The Gospel of John,* Volume I, by William Barclay (The Westminster Press, 1955, 1956); pages 72–74.

2. From http://www.fenstysforum.org/potpourr.htm

3. Quoted in *The Healing Fountain*, edited by Betty Thompson (General Board of Global Ministries, 1973); page 23.

Jesus and Zacchaeus: "Put It Behind You"

SCRIPTURE: Read Luke 19:1-10.

A rnold Palmer is not only one of the greatest golfers of all time, he is also the golfer who captured the hearts of people all over the world and paved the way for golf to become the popular sport it is today. Even Tiger Woods has said of him, "Arnold Palmer was what I wanted to be like." People by the hundreds followed him from hole to hole with great excitement, just like they do with Tiger Woods today. Palmer's loyal fans were called "Arnie's Army."

Today, if you go play a round of golf at the Rancho Park Golf Course in Los Angeles, you will see an interesting plaque just off the 17th hole, dedicated to Arnold Palmer. The plaque reads like this: "The first day of the 35th L.A. Open, Arnold Palmer, voted Golfer of the Year, took a 12 on this hole."

To this day, people tease Arnold Palmer about the time he shot a twelve on a par-four hole. Palmer just grins and says, "That plaque will be there long after I'm gone. But you have to put things like that behind you. That's one of the wonderful things about golf. Your next shot can be as good or as bad as your last one . . . but you'll always get another chance."[1]

This is not only true in golf, it is also true in life. That is what Zacchaeus discovered that day in Jericho long ago: We can have another chance. We can make a new start. With the help of God and by the grace of God, some things can be put behind us; and we can have a new beginning.

Some years ago, a little-known play entitled "Closed Because of Death" played off-Broadway in New York City. In this play, history comes to an end. Everybody dies. The earth is barren and seemingly is the symbol of defeat. But in the last act, the scene shifts to heaven. God is sitting there staring off into the future. He is holding a baby on his lap. Two angels pass by. One turns and says to the other, "He isn't going to start over again, is he? Doesn't he ever learn?" The second angel answers, "Well, you see, that is precisely the difference between God and us. God always sees a chance to start all over again."

That is, indeed, the good news of our faith, isn't it? And that is what the story of Zacchaeus is all about: the chance, with God's help, to start all over again. We Americans place a great emphasis on starting out on something. We make a big deal over starting out in a new position, a new marriage, a new career, or even a new house. There is something very exciting about starting out on those first few steps of a new journey.

The truth is, however, that some of life's greatest moments come, not when we start out, but when we start over. This is why we like the story of Zacchaeus so much. Jesus' encounter with Zacchaeus is the dramatic picture of how God can turn our lives around and give us a new beginning. Remember the story with me.

Jesus came that day into Jericho, the City of Palms. A great crowd awaited his arrival. People lined the streets in huge numbers. We can just imagine that the equivalent of the mayor and the city council were there with a key to the city, and the established church leaders were there to check out this traveling preacher who was causing such a stir.

Everybody was there. Some were devout believers. Some were there out of curiosity. Businesses were shut down. Schools were let out. Household chores were set aside. Everybody turned out—all of them on the streets, lining the way.

All of the people were not along the streets, however. One man was up in a tree. This man's name was Zacchaeus. He was a tax collector, and a dishonest one at that. (The practice of tax collectors often was to collect more than was actually owed and

28

then to pocket the profits for themselves.) If a popularity contest had been conducted in Jericho that day, Zacchaeus may well have come in dead last.

If you were asked to make a movie of the Zacchaeus story, whom would you pick to play Zacchaeus? A friend of mine says he would pick Danny DeVito! That is not a bad idea. Zacchaeus was the kind of character Danny DeVito often portrays. Zacchaeus was short in stature; and since he could not see over the crowd who had lined the streets to see Jesus, he had to be somewhat creative. If you will pardon the pun, Zacchaeus "rose to the occasion" by climbing a sycamore tree.

As Jesus came into the city of Jericho that day, he began to look at the faces in the crowd. His eyes found Zacchaeus, perched up in that tree, the picture of loneliness and rejection, the outcast of outcasts, the lowest of the lowly—and the heart of Jesus was touched. Jesus walked over, looked up, and said, "Zacchaeus, come down quickly. Let's have lunch together."

Now notice verse 7 of Luke 19. In the Revised Standard Version of the Bible, it starts off like this: "And when they saw it they all murmured" (Luke 19:7). That may be one of the most understated verses in the entire Bible. You can *bet* there was a murmur! The city officials were there. The leading citizens were there. The prominent business executives were there. The pillars of the church were there. And instead of having lunch with any of them, of all things, Jesus went to lunch with the Danny DeVito-type character of Jericho, the number one con man in town!

At this point in the story, there is a blank spot. We really do not know what happened at lunch. We do not know what was said in Zacchaeus's home. We do not know what transpired over the meal. But it must have been quite a power lunch . . . because Zacchaeus came out a changed man, a penitent man, a new man, a man ready to start over and do better. "Behold, Lord," he said, "the half of my goods I give to the poor; and if I have defrauded any one of anything, I restore it fourfold" (Luke 19:8, RSV).

Talk about a conversion; I mean, Zacchaeus was converted!

His soul was touched. His heart was warmed. Even his pocketbook got converted. Empowered by the love of Christ, Zacchaeus put the bad things he had done behind him and made a new start with his life.

Let me ask you something: Do you need to make a new start with your life? If so, there are some things that need to be left behind. That is what the Zacchaeus story teaches us. Through the love of Christ, you can have a new beginning; but for that to happen, you have to put some things behind you. Let me show you what I mean with three thoughts.

First of All, Put Selfishness Behind You

Have you heard the old joke about a small private airplane that was flying over the desert in the southwestern US one day? In addition to the pilot, those on board included a scientist, a minister, and a Boy Scout. Suddenly the plane began to sputter and falter. The pilot tried everything to stabilize the plane but gradually realized that it was hopeless. He came back to the three passengers and said, "I'm very sorry. I've done everything I know to do; but nothing has worked, and the plane is going down. Also, I have to inform you that a terrible mistake has been made; there are only three parachutes on board."

With that, the pilot grabbed a parachute and bailed out. The three remaining passengers looked at one another. Finally the scientist said, "Well, I have to be saved. I'm the most brilliant scientist in the world today. The world needs me and my bright mind." And with that, he bailed out.

That left the minister and the Boy Scout. The minister looked at the Boy Scout and said, "Look, son, I have lived a reasonably long life; and I am very grateful for it. You are still so young. You have most of your life before you. You take the last parachute and bail out. I insist." The Boy Scout smiled and said, "Well, Reverend, don't worry about a thing. We're both OK because, you see, the world's most brilliant scientist just jumped out of the plane with my knapsack on his back!"

Before Jesus Christ came into his life, Zacchaeus, had he been in a situation like that, would have been grabbing for the first parachute. He would selfishly have been thinking only of himself and his own interests. Remember how he had taken advantage of others. He had used others. He had cheated others. He had gotten rich at their expense. But then Christ came into his life that day in Jericho and turned his life around. Jesus Christ came into his life that day and loved him. And in that gracious act Jesus empowered Zacchaeus to put arrogant selfishness behind him and instead to take up the torch of love and graciousness and thoughtfulness and generosity toward others.

If you need to make a new start with your life, you need to put selfishness behind you. Christ is the One who can empower you to do just that.

Second, Put Prejudice Behind You

The word *prejudice* literally means "to pre-judge." It means to place narrow labels on people, to put people in boxes of our own making. Prejudice means not to see people as persons of value or as children of God or as our brothers and sisters. Prejudice means to see other people as adversaries to be "kept in their place" or used for our benefit.

Before Jesus Christ came into his life, that is what Zacchaeus was doing. He was looking at other people with lazy, harsh, greedy, prejudiced eyes and seeing them not as persons with feelings, not as God's beloved children, but rather as things to be used, as objects to take advantage of, as "marks" to use to get rich. But then along came Jesus; and Jesus, the Great Physician, opened Zacchaeus's eyes and enabled him to see people differently. Jesus took away the blinders of greed and prejudice and empowered Zacchaeus to see people with love and kindness and generosity.

Let me share with you a story about Francis of Assisi. When Francis turned his back on a wealthy, privileged life to serve God in simplicity, he took off his expensive robes, threw them aside, and walked out of the city. Along the way, he saw a leper on the side of the road. Francis passed him by. But then Francis remembered those powerful words of Jesus in Matthew 25, "Just as you did it to the least of these . . . you did it to me." Francis turned around, went back, and hugged the leper. Francis then continued his journey. He took a few steps and turned back to see the leper, but amazingly no one was there. Francis was convinced that the leper was Jesus in disguise.

Francis may well have been right because Jesus makes it clear in Matthew 25 that the best way to hug him is to hug our neighbor with unconditional love.

This was radical teaching for Jesus' time because the people back then believed in love, but theirs was a conditional love. They were more than glad to love those who looked like them and thought like them and acted like them and dressed like them. But they had no love at all for people who were different from them, like Gentiles or foreigners or lepers or tax collectors. And then along came Jesus with this strange new teaching: Love all people unconditionally. Love all people with no stipulations. Love all people with no strings attached.

When Jesus reached out to Zacchaeus and welcomed him into his life with open arms, that experience of being accepted by Jesus was so powerful that it opened Zacchaeus' eyes and enabled him to put his prejudiced ways behind him. He came down out of that sycamore tree reaching out to others, imitating the generous spirit of Jesus, imitating the unconditional love of our Lord.

Let me ask you something: Do you need to put prejudice behind you? Do you? If so, Christ is the one who can empower you to do just that.

Third and Finally, Put Loneliness Behind You

Before Christ came into his life, Zacchaeus was the picture of loneliness. But then Jesus reached out to him, and—Did you notice this?—he called Zacchaeus by name. He did not say, "Hey, you!" He called his name. He called him Zacchaeus and brought him into the circle of love.

We lost one of the finest members of our church recently. Her name was Randy. She was so young, just in her forties; but she packed so much life and love into those forty-plus years. She was so active in Sunday school. She had served on our board of

32

stewards. She had served on our finance committee, and she had served on our mission work trips. Three years ago she went to Russia and, as a single parent, adopted a beautiful little girl named Lara. Lara is three and a half years old now and already has made a special place for herself in our St. Luke's family.

On Memorial Day of 2002, Randy was diagnosed with cancer; and two months later, at two minutes after two o'clock in the afternoon, she passed out of this life into a new dimension of life with God in heaven. Randy was so loved in our church. She was a true friend to so many, and she had a sweetness of spirit that endeared her to all who knew her. I was so touched to see her friends there for her, around the clock. They took care of Randy with such beautiful, tender, compassionate Christian love.

On the day before she died, we promised Randy that we would take good care of her daughter, Lara. Randy said she wanted two things for Lara: for her to grow up in St. Luke's and for her to be a Girl Scout. We promised her that we would see that those things happened. I was so inspired by Randy's faith and courage and by the love in that room as we stood around Randy's hospital bed and held hands and prayed together.

Now, there is a name for that. It is *church,* and it is the best antidote there is for loneliness. That is what Jesus taught Zacchaeus that day long ago, and that is the message he has for you and me right now. So if you need to make a new start with your life, you need to put loneliness behind you and get in the church; and Christ is the One who can empower you to do just that.

Study / Discussion Questions

1. Discuss how it feels to start over again in a new job, a new home, a new relationship, a new town, or a new church. What is exciting about beginning a new journey? What may be intimidating or scary about it? Explain.

2. What lessons did you learn from the story of Zacchaeus? What is it about this story that you find the most interesting or the most remarkable?

3. List and discuss some of the causes and effects of selfishness. What examples can we find in Jesus Christ for overcoming selfishness?

4. In your own words, explain the meaning of the word *prejudice*. List some examples of prejudice, and share your thoughts about overcoming them.

5. Reflect on / discuss loneliness and its causes. Why is it so important to put loneliness behind you? What things in life does loneliness cause you to miss?

6. What do you want most to put behind you this Lenten season? How can God, your faith, and your church help you to start over?

Prayer

Dear God, thank you for the opportunity to start over. Help us to remember that you are the God of second chances. You want us to succeed in life and to have a relationship with you. Be with us as we look toward the future. Amen.

Focus for the Week

Enjoy a new beginning this week. Feel differently. Act differently. Forgive and forget. Give thanks for a fresh start. Forgive others as God has forgiven you. Help give a fresh start to others.

Notes

1. From *When Bad Things Happen to Good Golfers*, by Allan Zulla (Andrews McMeel, Publishing, 1998).

Jesus and Bartimaeus: "The Miracle of Love"

SCRIPTURE: Read Mark 10:46-52.

D
r. Brian Bauknight tells of a recent national survey in which people were asked the question, "What words would you most like to hear spoken to you in genuine sincerity?" Three answers came to the top of the list. What do you think they were? How would you answer that question? What are the words you would most like to hear?

Answer number one was, "I love you." The second most popular answer was, "I forgive you." And the third, interestingly, was, "Supper is ready." All three of these sought-after phrases are fascinating; but for now I want us to focus on the number one answer, "I love you"—the miracle of love. What does "love" mean? How would you define it?

Some months ago, a group of professional people posed this question, "What does love mean?" to a group of children who ranged in age from four to eight. Their answers were poignant, humorous, and touching.

Rebecca, age 8, said, "When my grandmother got arthritis, she couldn't bend over and paint her toenails anymore. So my grandfather does it for her all the time, even when his hands got arthritis too. That's love."

Billy, age 4, said this: "When someone loves you, the way they say your name is different. You know that your name is safe in their mouth."

Noelle, age 7, put it like this: "Love is when you tell a guy you like his shirt, then he wears it every day."

Chrissy, age 6, had this to say: "Love is when you go out to eat and give somebody most of your French fries without making them give you any of theirs."

Danny, age 7, defined love like this: "Love is when my mommy makes coffee for my daddy and she takes a sip before giving it to him, to make sure the taste is OK."

Mary Ann, age 4, said, "Love is when your puppy licks your face even after you left him alone all day."

And then this last one: Karl, age 5, said, "Love is when a girl puts on perfume and a boy puts on shaving cologne and they go out and smell each other."[1]

Aren't children wonderful? Their attempts to define love are terrific, but the truth is that it is very difficult to find words big enough to capture the full spectrum of what love is. The miracle of love is so amazing that dictionary definitions do not quite measure up.

Love can be demonstrated, however; and that is precisely what Jesus does for us in this encounter recorded in Mark 10. He demonstrates Christian love, the kind of love needed in our homes; in our marriages; in our churches; in our friendships; and in our interpersonal relationships with coworkers, neighbors, acquaintances, and even strangers. In this powerful story that describes the healing of Bartimaeus, we see a portrait of Christian love. Remember the story with me.

Jesus was on his way to Jerusalem. He was on his way to the cross when he encountered this man, Bartimaeus. Bartimaeus, who was blind, was sitting by the roadside in Jericho. He was doing what he did daily: He was begging for money. Obviously he had heard about Jesus. Bartimaeus sensed that this was his moment, his chance. So when Jesus came near, Bartimaeus began to cry out urgently, "Jesus, son of David, have mercy on me!" (Mark 10:47).

The crowd tried to shush him. They thought Jesus was too busy and too important to be bothered with the likes of Bartimaeus, this poor, wretched, blind beggar. But Bartimaeus would not be denied. He would not be shushed. No! He cried out, more desperately, "Son of David, have mercy on me!" (Mark 10:48). Suddenly Jesus stopped. He turned around.

36

Somehow, over the noise of the crowd, he heard the poignant cry of Bartimaeus; and Jesus called for him. "Take heart," people shouted; "get up, he is calling you" (10:49). Then Bartimaeus threw his cloak aside. He sprang up and made his way through the crowd and came into the presence of Jesus.

Notice here that Jesus was not presumptuous or arrogant or possessive. Jesus never romped and stomped on people. He did not force himself on people. He did not pompously pronounce what Bartimaeus needed. No, he was very low-key. Humbly he asked Bartimaeus, "What do you want me to do for you?" (Mark 10:51a). Bartimaeus answered, "My teacher, let me see again" (10:51b). Then Jesus said to him, "Go; your faith has made you well" (10:52b). The Scriptures tell us that the blind man Bartimaeus then received his sight, and he followed Jesus on the way.

What can we learn from this powerful story? There is so much here. Obviously we could go in a number of different directions. For example, we could look at the matter of healing, how Jesus healed Bartimaeus and how healing happens today. Or we could talk about the special qualities of Bartimaeus that jump out of this story: his persistence, his perseverance, his boldness, his determination, his sensitivity to the uniqueness of the moment, his faith, his unwillingness to give in to the fear of embarrassment, his ability to seize an opportunity. Or we could point out that in this great story we have the good news of our faith summed up in three points: our need, God's action, and our response.

> *Our need*—we, like Bartimaeus, are blind and needy.
> *God's action*—God can heal us and restore our sight and give us a new vision.
> *Our response*—like Bartimaeus, we can follow Jesus on the way.

There is so much here in this great story. But for now, I want us to zero in on what this story teaches us about *love*. Love is a many-splendored thing! We see that graphically in this touching encounter between Jesus and Bartimaeus. Let me list for your consideration a few of the qualities of Christian love suggested by this story. I am sure you will think of others.

First of All, Love Notices

Jesus was so perceptive, so aware of what was going on around him; and he heard the cries of Bartimaeus. Someone might say, "Well, of course he heard the cries. Bartimaeus was shouting as loudly as he could, screaming at the top of his lungs!" But let me paint the picture of that scene.

The time was several days before Passover. The law dictated that every male Jew over twelve years of age was to go to Jerusalem for Passover. So as this story in Mark 10 begins, thousands of pilgrims are making their way to Jerusalem. The setting is Jericho, a town about fifteen miles northeast of Jerusalem. Jericho is situated on one of the main highways leading to the Holy City.

For all the thousands of pilgrims heading toward Jerusalem, there were thousands more being left behind: the young, the women, the servants, the physically challenged, the poor. It was these people, those being left behind, who were lining the street to cheer the pilgrims as they passed by. Picture a big parade or an airport pep rally for the home team as they leave for the big championship game. The scene was loud and boisterous and festive, a lot of people and a lot going on—songs, chants, cheers, the tramping of feet—just a lot of booming crowd noise. Amazingly, despite the chaos and confusion generated by all the people on and beside the highway, Jesus heard Bartimaeus's cry. He took notice of the pain and the urgency in Bartimaeus's voice. Jesus stopped. He called for Bartimaeus, and he healed him.

Put that over against this: Bob Edmunds tells a story of what it feels like to be overlooked and ignored. He and his family were vacationing one summer and decided to worship at a prominent church in a large metropolitan area. This church had quite a reputation for great preaching and powerful music. Bob and his wife were impressed by the worship service. The sermon was riveting, and the music was inspiring. The worship service did not disappoint them, but the lack of hospitality did.

From the moment they arrived at that church to the time they left, not one person noticed them, not one person spoke to them, not one person greeted them or welcomed them. No one directed them to the nursery. They had to find it for themselves. No one invited them to the fellowship hall for coffee and refreshments afterward. They had to find it on their own. In fact, Bob deliberately stood underneath the huge chandelier in the center of that spacious hall for at least five minutes, gazing up at it and looking as conspicuous as possible. But no one noticed. No one came up to him or introduced himself or herself to him. "We felt as though we were invisible," Bob said. "That church was as cold and lifeless as a corpse. I don't care how good the preaching and music were. Nothing could make up for their lack of hospitality. No one noticed that we were even there."[2]

Let me ask you something: Would you have noticed? Would you have been perceptive enough to realize what that family needed? Would you have reached out to help them? That is the first attribute of love. It sees and hears problems to solve, people to help, and opportunities to serve. Love notices. That is number one.

Second, Love Includes

There is an old story about the man who owned and operated a country store in a small, family-oriented community. It was the kind of store where people came to visit with one another and to play checkers beside the potbelly stove. The storeowner had an unusual practice. Every time he made a sale, he quoted a verse of Scripture appropriate for the particular customer who had just bought something. At this point, like an E.F. Hutton commercial, the checker players would stop their game and their conversation to hear what Scripture verse he would quote.

For example, if a child bought some candy, the storeowner would say, "Let the children come to me. Of such is the kingdom of God." Or if an older couple purchased something, he would say, "Honor your father and mother that your days may be long in the land which the Lord your God gives you."

One day a bright gold Cadillac pulled up in front of the store. It was pulling a very expensive horse trailer. The Cadillac had out-of-state license plates. The owner of the gold Cadillac came in and asked the storeowner if he had any horse blankets. "Yes sir," was the reply. The storeowner went to the back of the store to his stack of horse blankets and pulled one off the top. It was bright red in color. He brought it back to the front. The horse owner asked, "How much?" The storeowner replied, "Twenty-five dollars." The horse owner said, "Now wait a minute. My horse is a thoroughbred. I can't put a twenty-five-dollar blanket on this fine animal. I want something more expensive."

The storeowner went back to the same stack of blankets and pulled out a green one. "Now that's more like it," said the horse owner. "How much?" "One hundred dollars" came the reply. "No, no," said the horse owner. "My horse is one of the finest horses in America. He has to have the most expensive blanket you've got."

The storeowner went back to the same stack of blankets a third time, and this time he pulled out a blue blanket. "Now we're talking," said the horse owner. "How much is this one?" "Two thousand dollars," said the storeowner. "That's perfect," answered the horse owner. He pulled out two thousand dollars, paid for the blanket, left the store, and drove off. The men playing checkers stopped their game. They could not wait to hear what Bible verse the storeowner would quote this time. He rang open the cash register; inserted the two thousand dollars; and said, "He was a stranger, and I took him in!"

Bartimaeus was a stranger to Jesus, but Jesus did not take him in; he brought him in. Jesus brought him into the circle of love.

I have a friend who does a beautiful thing. I have seen him do it so many times. It is a gesture that is just as natural to him as breathing. If he is in conversation with a group of people and you walk up, he will immediately step back and open the circle. Then he will reach back gently with his arm and bring you in. He is so gracious and thoughtful in this way. He notices your arrival and welcomes you into the group. He includes you immediately. Do you know what people say about him? They say, "He is the most Christlike person I know!" That is what love does, and that is what Jesus did for Bartimaeus that day. Jesus brought him into the circle of love.

Most people in Jesus' day would not have done that. They would have said about Bartimaeus, "He's blind, so don't have anything to do with him. He must have done something terrible to get himself in that fix. He is under the judgment of God, so steer clear of him. Let him sit over there on the side of the road and beg for pennies, but don't let him into our polite society. Toss him a coin or two if you want to, but it's really best to ignore him and shun him."

They did not even like it when Bartimaeus called out to Jesus; they tried to silence him. "Hush up, Bartimaeus! Don't bother the Master. He doesn't have time for the likes of you." But they were oh so wrong, weren't they? That day in Jericho, Jesus showed them they were wrong. He showed them and us that first, love notices and second, love includes.

Third and Finally, Love Redeems

To *redeem* means to rescue, to deliver, to save. It means to convert a bad situation into a good situation. It means to turn a defeat into a victory. That is what Jesus did for Bartimaeus. Jesus noticed him, included him, and redeemed him.

Two brothers lived on adjoining farms. They had farmed side by side for forty years. They had shared information and machinery and helped each other in every way. But then one day there was a misunderstanding. It was just a little thing, but it festered and grew into a major difference and finally exploded into an exchange of bitter words . . . and then weeks of silence.

One morning there was a knock on the door of the older brother's home. John opened the door to find a man with a carpenter's toolbox. "I'm looking for a few days' work," the carpenter said. "Maybe you have a few small jobs here and there I could help you with?" "Yes," said John. "I do have a job for you. See that farm on the other side of the creek? That's my neighbor; in fact, it's my younger brother. You won't believe what he did. Last week there was just a meadow between us; but he took his bulldozer to the river levee, and now there is a creek between us. I think he did it to spite me, but I'll show him. See that pile of lumber there by the barn? I want you to take that lumber and build me a fence—an eight-foot fence, so I won't need to see his place or his face ever again." The carpenter said, "I think I understand the situation. Show me the nails and the post-hole digger, and I'll get started. I am sure I can do a job that will please you." The older brother got the carpenter started, and then he was off for the day to take care of business in town.

At sunset, the older brother returned home and was amazed to see that the carpenter, who had just finished the job, had not built a fence at all. Rather, he had built a beautiful bridge, a bridge stretching from one side of the creek to the other. It was a fine piece of work, handrails and all. The neighbor, the younger brother, was coming across the bridge with a big smile on his face and his hand outstretched. "John," he said, "you are quite a fellow to build this bridge after all I've said and done." The two brothers met in the middle of the bridge. They shook hands. They both apologized. Then they hugged each other, and a bad situation was redeemed. They turned to see the carpenter hoist his toolbox on his shoulder and turn to leave. "Wait a minute!" the brothers shouted. "Please stay with us. We've got a lot more projects for you." "I'd love to stay on," said the carpenter, "but I must move on now. I have lots more bridges to build."

Look at how the Bartimaeus story ends. Do not miss this. The last verse reads, "And immediately Bartimaeus regained his sight, and he followed Jesus on the way" (Mark 10:52, adapted). Redeemed by Christ's love, Bartimaeus became a disciple. He went with Jesus to help the carpenter of Nazareth build more bridges of love.

Study / Discussion Questions

1. Discuss what it means when someone says, "I love you." How do people respond to love? How does love have the power to change persons?

2. Has your idea of what *love* is changed over time? Explain your answer.

3. Reflect on / discuss the meaning of the author's statement that "love notices."

4. List and discuss ways to make people—whether strangers or friends—feel included. Share a time when you were grateful to be included.

5. In your own words, explain what it means to be redeemed. At the end of the Bartimaeus story, how was Bartimaeus redeemed by Christ's love?

Prayer

Dear God, thank you for the miracle of love and for your love for us. Open our eyes to the needs of others, and help us to follow Jesus Christ's example in loving them. In his name we pray. Amen.

Focus for the Week

Practice love in action this week. Take notice of others, and go out of your way to include people. Meditate on the redeeming power of love and on how you have been changed by God's love through Jesus Christ. Open your eyes to see miracles of love this week.

Notes

1. Copyright © 1999-2003 Ahmad Anvari Anvari.org (http://www.anvari.org/fun/Truth/What_is_Love.html)

2. Thanks to Bret Blair, e-sermons.com, June 30, 2003, quoting a sermon by Reverend J. Scott Miller entitled "Ministry of Hospitality."

Jesus and Mary and Martha: "Dangerous Attitudes"

SCRIPTURE: *Read Luke 10:38-42.*

Some years ago, the Archbishop of Canterbury was rushing to catch a train in London. In his haste he accidentally jumped onto the wrong passenger car and found himself in a car full of patients from a mental hospital. They were all dressed in hospital clothing.

Just as the train pulled out of the station, an orderly came in and began to count the patients, "1, 2, 3, 4 . . . " when suddenly he saw this distinguished looking gentleman there wearing a business suit and a clerical collar. He asked, "Who are you?" The answer came back, "I am the Archbishop of Canterbury!" And the orderly responded, " . . . 5, 6, 7, 8 . . . "

The point of that story is this: It is so important to know who we are and who other people are. If we know what makes us tick and what makes other people tick, we get along better. If we understand where we are coming from and where other people are coming from, we relate better. There is more compassion, more empathy, and more kindness.

That is why in recent years we have heard so much about personality tests. Employers, counselors, and job-placement agencies are using them effectively. We are working on a plan right now at our church to use a personality profile to help members find their special place of ministry in our church. It occurred to me that this method of personality testing would be an interesting way to study a passage of Scripture. We will try this together as we look at the somewhat confusing story of Mary and Martha in Luke 10.

Dr. Roger Birkman, a Houston psychologist, has developed a fascinating computer personality profile that suggests, broadly speaking, that there are four different personality styles. I will outline them for us. See if you can find yourself or someone you know somewhere between the lines.

First, there is *the autocratic doer*. This person is action-oriented and strong-willed. This person means business, and everybody else had better get out of the way.

Second, there is *the detailed planner*. This person plans the work and then "works the plan." The detailed planner's personality is precisely what the name implies—one who thinks things through in great detail; one who plans ahead; one who wants things done neatly, orderly, and systematically. The detailed planner does really well, as long as no one messes up the plan.

The third personality style, according to Dr. Birkman, is *the enthusiastic salesperson*. This person has no plan. The enthusiastic salesperson is a "people person" who operates on personality and has the strong ability to wow people and win them over and to sell them on his or her ideas and dreams.

A fourth personality style suggested by the Birkman profile is *the artistic poetic philosophe*r. This person is more soulful, more tuned in to beauty, reverence, and awe. The artistic poetic philosopher is creative—one who enjoys quiet and pensive moments of solitude, one who can tune in to the wonders of the universe, one who can experience a sunset or a Brahms melody and feel in that experience the presence of God nearer than breathing.

Roger Birkman has developed an interesting way of clarifying these four personality styles, so that we can recognize them more quickly and easily. He says, "Imagine that you have nine cats in a house and that your task is to get the cats out of the house. How would you do it?"

How would the autocratic doer handle this? Well, obviously the autocratic doer would take charge and say, "Scat!" and the cats had better get out if they know what is good for them!

The detailed planner, on the other hand, would number the cats—1, 2, 3, 4, 5, 6, 7, 8, 9—in calligraphy, with neat tags attached to the right side of each cat's collar. Then the detailed planner would make nine neat holes in the wall and number them 1 through 9 in calligraphy. Cat 1 must go out Hole 1; Cat 2 must go out Hole 2; Cat 3 must go out Hole 3; and if Cat 4 runs out through Hole 7, then the detailed planner's whole world is thrown out of whack!

The enthusiastic salesperson would say, "No problem; piece of cake. I can handle this." Then the enthusiastic salesperson would open all the doors and windows; get some warm milk and cat food; go outside; and say, "Here, Kitty, Kitty!" and convince the cats that they would be a lot better off outside anyway!

Meanwhile, the artistic poetic philosopher would say, "What in the world am I doing worrying about cats?"

The point for us of Roger Birkman's personality profile is obvious: We are different; and when we recognize, understand, respect, and celebrate our differences, we get along better. This idea is deeply rooted in the Bible. It is one of the key themes of Paul's first letter to the church at Corinth. Some of us are prophets, and some of us are teachers. Some of us are action-oriented, while others of us are pensive and thoughtful. Some of us are poetic, and some of us are autocratic. Some of us are loud, and some of us are quiet.

We are different people with different personalities, different styles, different temperaments. And that is OK! Indeed, it is beautiful, as long as we are loving and tolerant about it.[1]

With this as a backdrop for our thinking, look with me at this remarkable passage in Luke 10 where Jesus comes to visit in the home of Mary and Martha. Put on your amateur psychologist's hat and see if you can psychoanalyze Mary and Martha to figure out what their personality styles are and how their personality styles impact the situation.

Here is the story. All morning long there has been a bustle of excitement in the home in Bethany. Jesus is coming for dinner! Martha is so excited. Since daybreak, she has been sweeping, scrubbing, dusting, checking recipes, darting in and out of the kitchen, frantically preparing the food, and putting the place in order for this special occasion.

Every moment now is precious. Time is "a-wasting." So much to do! So many details to cover! Then Jesus arrives, and look what happens. Mary whisks in to take over as hostess. She welcomes Jesus and the disciples warmly and ushers them into the living room. There is a certain urgency about the moment. The Master is on his way to Jerusalem and the cross. He begins to talk to his friends. He has so much to tell them, so much to teach them, and so little time.

They listen attentively, especially Mary. Mary has positioned herself at the feet of Jesus, and she is drinking in his every word. How good to have him here! How good to hear him again! How good it is just to be in his presence!

Meanwhile, Martha is out in the kitchen, slaving away—preparing the meal, polishing the silverware, cutting up the fruits and vegetables, checking the last-minute details, doing the one hundred and one things that in her super-efficient mind need to be done.

Here is the problem, however: All this time while Martha is working feverishly, she is seething inside! Her indignation mounts. She is getting more and more aggravated, more and more frustrated. She feels more and more put upon, more and more stressed out. *Where is Mary?* she wonders. *Why isn't she in here helping me? Who does she think she is, sitting in there with our guests and leaving all the dirty work to me? Surely Jesus can see the injustice of this situation!* Martha reasons.

Finally, unable to contain herself any longer, her resentment erupts. She bursts out of the kitchen into the living room and makes a scene! Have you ever been in a scene before? Martha makes one here. She cries, "Look at this, Lord! I'm having to do all the work here! Don't you care that my sister, Mary, has left me to serve alone? You get on to her now! Tell her to get out here in the kitchen and help me!"

Jesus says to her, "Martha, Martha, don't be so worried and troubled about so many things. Relax. Lighten up. There is need of only one thing. Mary has chosen the good portion, which will not be taken away from her." End of story.

Now look at these personality styles. Have you figured them out? What about Mary? Do you have her pegged? Well, of course, she is the artistic poetic philosopher, who is thrilled just to bask in the warmth of that moment. She is stirred, thrilled, touched, and inspired by the presence of Jesus.

How about Martha? Well, obviously, she is the detailed planner. She has planned this event to the nth degree. She has covered every detail. She has worked her fingers to the bone in her super-efficient way. Yet, here in the story, Jesus rebukes Martha. It is a gentle rebuke; but, nevertheless, he did speak words that compared Martha unfavorably with her less practical sister, Mary. And the question that explodes out of this story is, *Why?*

Not for a moment should we imagine that Jesus was unappreciative of Martha's intense desire for a job well done. Not for a moment should we imagine that Jesus Christ thinks artistic poetic philosophers are better than detailed planners.

No! Not that at all. If Mary had been seething, he would have rebuked her. You see, Jesus was not concerned about what Martha was doing outwardly; he was concerned about what she was feeling inwardly! His concern was for Martha herself! He was concerned about her attitudes! How perceptive he was. How quickly he could size things up. In a moment, with a brief glance, he could penetrate right down into the innermost motives. He could see right down into the inner recesses of a person's soul. Let me stress again that this is no criticism of detailed-planner personalities. We *need* them. Every church, every business, every family needs Marthas. We need detailed-planner personalities.

When Jesus looked at Martha that day in that emotional scene, however, he saw some red flags, some warning signals, some danger signs, some destructive attitudes within her that were more harmful to Martha herself than to anyone else. Jesus loved Martha. They were good friends; and that day he saw in her some hurtful attitudes that were working within her like "spiritual poisons," petty attitudes that can devastate and destroy the soul.

Let's look together at these dangerous attitudes that were present within Martha. We may find ourselves, or someone we know, somewhere between the lines.

First, When Jesus Looked at Martha That Day, He Saw Deep Down Inside of Her the Dangerous Attitude of Resentment

Martha was resenting Mary. In my opinion, there is nothing more destructive to our spiritual lives than resentment. It can absolutely ruin our lives, and Jesus knew it. It concerned him to see this dangerous attitude of resentment in Martha.

In the Greek language, there are two words for anger. There is *thumos*—a kind of "quick anger" that quickly blazes up and just as quickly dies down. And then there is *orge* (pronounced or-GAY). This is a kind of "seething anger," a brooding anger, an anger that is long-lived. It is the anger of the person who nurses his or her wrath to keep it warm, an anger that festers and will not die. That is *orge*—a seething, burning, brooding anger—and that is what resentment is made of.

In the Sermon on the Mount (Matthew 5–7), Jesus talked repeatedly about the dangers of resentment; and he said, in effect,

Beware of resentment; it is dangerous!
Beware of brooding, seething anger!
Beware of resentful gossip!
Beware of the contemptuous, resentful tone or attitude!

All of these are murderous; all of these are devastating.

We see it here in the Mary and Martha story in a couple of dramatic ways:

First, notice the words used to describe Martha, three words: *distracted, anxious, troubled*. That is what resentment does to you!

Even more, however, Martha's resentment cut her off, not only from her sister, Mary, but also from her Lord. The same thing happened to the older brother in the parable of the prodigal son. He resented his younger brother, and it cut him off from the father.

That is how resentment affects us, and that is why it is so dangerous. It separates us from people, and it separates us from God!

In the story of Mary and Martha, what is Jesus saying? Simply this: Beware of the dangerous attitude of resentment. It can devastate your soul!

Second, When Jesus Looked at Martha That Day, He Saw Deep Down Inside of Her the Dangerous Attitude of Narrowness

Martha was done in by her own narrow perspective. Martha thought her way was the only way, and she wanted to force her way on Mary!

Martha's view had become so narrow that she could not see any way to receive the Master but her way. She was blind to the miracle of uniqueness. She forgot that we are all different, that we are individuals, and that each of us has a unique relationship with our Lord.

How often I have seen this "narrow attitude" cause problems theologically. Some people think *their* religious experience is the only valid one, and they try to force their way on everybody they meet. They do not understand that God is big enough to relate to each one of us differently, individually, uniquely, personally.

Let me illustrate. Some years ago, I went to a party in recognition of a married couple's outstanding work in the church's youth program. Let me tell you about this couple. I will call them Betty and Bill. They had very different personalities.

Betty was vivacious, outgoing, gregarious, affectionate, a hugger. If you gave her a bow ribbon, she would jump up and down and squeal with delight and then run around and hug and kiss everybody in the room.

Bill, on the other hand, was the opposite. He was quiet, reserved, shy, stable, balanced. If you gave him a Mercedes and a trip to Hawaii, all he would do is say quietly and sincerely, "Thank you."

On this particular night, we gave Betty and Bill a surprise party. The guests jumped out from their hiding places, shouted "Surprise!" and then gave Betty and Bill a present. It was a beautiful plaque.

51

Do you know what Betty did? She read the plaque out loud. She squealed with delight. She cried. She jumped up and down and then ran around the room hugging and kissing everybody in sight. Meanwhile, Bill waited. When Betty was finished, he said quietly, "I want to thank you also!"

That is not the end of the story, however. Betty got mad at Bill, and in front of all the guests she made a scene.

"Look at you, Bill. You don't appreciate anything. If you did, you would *act* like it. You would do like I do!"

But, you see, Bill cannot act that way. He is just not made that way. He is not wired the same way Betty is. He cannot act like her, cannot respond that way. If he did, it would be fake, artificial, embarrassing. I wanted to say, "Betty, leave him alone. Don't force your way on him. Let him do it his way. Let him be Bill!" I have to tell you that I enjoyed Betty's appreciative hugs and kisses; but I also knew that Bill's quiet "Thank you" was just as real, just as genuine, just as valid.

In this episode with Mary and Martha, Jesus was saying, "Beware of the dangerous attitude of narrowness. It can devastate your soul."

Third and Finally, When Jesus Looked at Martha That Day, He Saw Deep Down Inside of Her the Dangerous Attitude of Unkindness

Do not miss this point. When will we ever learn? Martha tried to make herself look good by making Mary look bad; but it "boomeranged" on her, and she came off (at least in this instance) as the unpleasant one. Ultimately, it happens every time. Our harsh, condemning judgments come back to haunt us. When we are unkind to others, we are the ones who end up looking bad.

Some time ago, I read an article on marriage. It was rather ordinary, except for one great statement, one of the greatest statements about marital relationships I have ever heard or read. It said this:

> If you are ever in a situation where you have to choose between making either yourself or your mate look good,

ALWAYS CHOOSE TO MAKE YOUR MATE LOOK GOOD RATHER THAN YOURSELF!

Jesus would have liked that counsel; and he would have enhanced it by saying, "Always choose to make other people look good rather than yourself!"

That kind of kindness "boomerangs" too. It comes back to bless. I know a woman who lives like that—always bragging on others and encouraging others, always making others look good rather than herself. The fascinating thing is that everybody who knows her loves her and respects her and appreciates her and admires her because of her unwavering kindness.

The point is clear: What we send out comes back! If we send out unkindness, it comes back to haunt us. If we send out grace and love and compassion, those come back to bless us.

In the Mary and Martha story, Jesus is teaching us a great lesson about our inner attitudes; and he is saying, Beware of resentment, beware of narrowness, and beware of unkindness. Choose instead the way of grace and love and compassion.

Study / Discussion Questions

1. Why is it often difficult to recognize dangerous attitudes within yourself? What are some of the warning signs of dangerous attitudes?

2. Reflect on / share a dangerous attitude that you sometimes have and how you try to control it.

3. How would you describe your personality? How does your personality help or hinder you as a Christian? Give an example.

4. If you resent someone, what does that say about you and what is inside your heart? Whom does resentment hurt the most and in what ways?

5. What causes people to see things from a narrow perspective? What do they miss seeing as a result?

6. List and discuss some of the motivations for unkindness. How do both unkindness and kindness "boomerang" at times?

Prayer

Dear God, thank you for the ability to choose our own attitudes. May we choose positive and loving attitudes that show others your love. Keep us aware of dangerous attitudes and the damage they can cause. Help us to treat people as Jesus treated others and as we wish to be treated ourselves. Amen.

Focus for the Week

Strive for grace, love, and compassion this week. Become more aware of dangerous attitudes in self and others. Consider how your attitude can change your life and the lives of others. Be a healer this week.

Note

1. Adapted from *Can You Remember to Forget?* by James W. Moore (Abingdon Press, 1991); pages 40–43. Also see *True Colors*, by Roger W. Birkman (Birkman International, Inc.).

Jesus and Judas: "Why Did Judas Betray?"

SCRIPTURE: *Read Mark 14:43-50.*

Some years ago, a young lawyer called me one morning to ask a favor. He wanted me to visit one of his clients, who at that moment was behind bars, in jail awaiting trial for armed robbery.

When the lawyer said the prisoner's name, I recognized it immediately. There had been quite a bit of discussion and information about him in the newspapers and on television. He was from somewhere out west. The media had portrayed him as mean, wicked, ruthless, evil, unfeeling, and uncaring. He looked the part. His complexion was ruddy, rough, and weather-beaten. His eyes were bleary. He had this cold, glassy-eyed stare, probably produced from too many drugs and too much alcohol. His arms were covered with cheap-looking tattoos, and his hair looked like a disheveled mass of dried straw. He was a tough-looking character. He would have scared the wits out of Hannibal Lecter!

Even though he was handcuffed, I must confess that I felt a little uneasy as I was locked in his prison cell with him. I can remember it as if it were yesterday, the sound of that cell door slamming shut and being locked and the jailor walking away and leaving me alone—all alone—with this hardened criminal.

I introduced myself and told him that his lawyer had sent me. He just glared at me with a fierce stare. There was a period of awkward silence, which lasted only a few seconds; but it seemed like an eternity. Not really knowing what to say to this man or how I might help him, I simply blurted out, "Why don't you tell me your story?" And he did. He started slowly, but soon the words were flowing easily as the truth of his story came out.

His father had beaten him unmercifully when he was a little boy. He had lots of scars to show for it. When he was eight years old, his father had deserted the family. His mother, from that point on, began to entertain a succession of men in their home. When he was about ten years old, his mother taught him how to steal and encouraged him to take anything he could get his hands on.

Later, as he entered his teen years, his mother turned him against every symbol of authority and responsibility. She taught him to hate the school, the church, and the law. When he was fourteen, his father returned home briefly and in an alcoholic rage almost killed both mother and child. He and his mother were taken to a charity hospital. When he was well enough, he slipped out of the hospital and ran away. To survive, he did the only thing he knew how to do—rob and steal.

On and on he went with the tragic details of his story. As I listened to him, I had a strange mixture of feelings. I did not feel so afraid of him anymore. I felt sorry for him. He had committed a long series of serious crimes in several states over a period of many years. He needed to be in prison. I knew that, and he knew that. The community needed to be protected from him. In fact, he told me that day that he wanted to be there! He had come to realize that he really needed and craved some sort of strong supervision.

Here was a man who, because of his traumatic early years, was now consumed with anger, was now a menace to himself and to his community, and was now unable to recall a single moment of any tenderness at all in his life. Here was a man who now actually wanted to spend the rest of his years in prison. That is what he wanted to talk to me about. He wanted to tell a minister his story. He wanted to tell a minister about this decision he had made to ask to be put behind bars for life. It was his way of trying to say, "I'm sorry." It was his way of trying to rectify and redeem a horrible situation. As I listened to him, I made an important discovery that day: Everybody has a story to tell; and when you hear their story, you will feel differently toward them!

Shortly after that experience, I saw a movie about the arrest, trial, and crucifixion of Jesus. It was a bit overdone for my taste, but I remember how dramatically the character of Judas was portrayed. He was the heavy! From the very first moment, you knew beyond a shadow of a doubt that he was the bad guy. When he betrayed Jesus later in the movie, you expected it. When he took his own life, you were convinced that it was an appropriate and fitting end for this evil character. But then, as with that man in the jail cell, I found myself wondering about Judas. I yearned to ask him, "Judas, what is your story? Judas, what is the real truth of your story?"

We are often reluctant to ask that question, aren't we? We much prefer that people come to us, not with a story, but in simple caricature! We want to know whether a person is a good guy or a bad guy. "Does he wear a white hat or a black hat?" We are uncomfortable when someone says, "Well, it's not all that simple."

Have you heard about the man who was looking for a one-handed lawyer? "A one-handed lawyer?" asked his friend, "How come?" The reply was brusque: "I am looking for an attorney who won't say, 'On the one hand this, but on the other hand that!' I want a 'one-handed' lawyer."

I suppose we all want that: simple explanations for complex problems. We want a world where no one is just "so-so," a world where everyone is either good or bad. Some of the early Christian writers were probably like that in regard to Judas. They probably did not tell his story. They told *their* story about him, and they made of him a simplistic caricature—a bad guy! They painted him as a dramatically evil and wicked man; and history has dealt with him even more harshly, to the point where today no name carries such shame as that of Judas Iscariot. There is no feeling of sympathy toward him at all, almost to the point where we wonder if perhaps history has made him the scapegoat for the terrible things that happened to Jesus as he was arrested, tried, and crucified.

I keep wondering, *What is Judas's story? What is the real truth* of Judas's story? *Why did he betray his Master?* Over the years, many answers have emerged. Let's brainstorm about them and see how many we can list.

Why did Judas betray? Did he do it for money? Some have suggested this explanation, saying that Judas was undone by his greed and his love for money. But this argument really does not carry much weight because Judas could have struck a better bargain than he did—thirty pieces of silver (Matthew 26:14-15)—if his interest had been money. Remember also that almost immediately after Jesus was arrested, Judas threw the money back at those who had given it to him and then took his own life (Matthew 27:3-5). Some say Judas betrayed Jesus for the money, but I do not think it was that simple.

Was Judas a spy? Some have said that. They think Judas was "planted" among Jesus' close followers by the authorities of the day, placed there from the beginning to betray Jesus at just the right time. I do not know how you feel about this "cloak and dagger" idea; but, again, to me it seems too simple an explanation, more of a caricature than a real story.

Was it predestined that Judas should be the traitor? Was it predetermined that Judas would be the one to betray his Master? Some have said that is the explanation. "It was written in the cards. It was all part of the plan."

How do you feel about that? Do you agree with that? If you do, then how do you balance that with God's grace and with God's gift of freedom of choice? Did Judas have a choice? Or was he predestined to betray? What do you think?

Still others say that **perhaps there was a political strategy on Judas's part.** Maybe Judas was simply trying to force the issue, to bring the showdown, to make Jesus act, to make Jesus go ahead and bring the Kingdom with power. Judas might have reasoned, *I'll call his hand. I'll set it up. I'll put him in a position where he has no choice but to react with force and move to establish his kingdom. And when it's all over and done, he will thank me for it!* What do you think? Do you think this was what was going on in the mind of Judas? Many bright scholars have believed this to be the case.

But still others think that **Judas just got scared** and acted out of fear. The tides were turning against them. There was a groundswell of opposition, and the opponents of Jesus were formidable. *Why did Jesus have to cause such a stir in the Temple? When he overturned the moneychangers' tables and cleansed the Temple, he stepped on some mighty big toes,* Judas may have thought. *They are really out to get him now, and I could go down with him—"guilt by association."* Maybe Judas got scared and sold out simply to save his own skin.

Or **maybe Judas just misunderstood Jesus** and missed the whole point of who Jesus was and what he was trying to do. I rather suspect that we often do that, too. We betray Jesus because we miss the whole point of who he was and what he was trying to do. Let me show you what I mean.

Judas Missed the Message

And sometimes, so do we. On December 17, 1903, Orville and Wilbur Wright (with Orville at the controls) kept their hand-built airplane up in the air for twelve seconds. It was an incredible accomplishment. As one humorous version of the story goes, they sent a telegram to their sister in Dayton, Ohio, which read something like this:

FIRST SUSTAINED FLIGHT TODAY. HOPE TO BE HOME FOR CHRISTMAS.

The excited sister took the incredible news to the local newspaper editor. The next morning, though, to her shock and dismay, the headline read in bold letters,

POPULAR LOCAL BICYCLE MERCHANTS TO BE HOME FOR HOLIDAYS!

Incredible news—one of the biggest news stories in all of history—and it passed Dayton by that day because the editor had missed the message. How often that happens. We miss the message.

Jesus came preaching love, not force; forgiveness, not vengeance; mercy, not cruelty; kindness, not hatred. We, like

Judas, are still missing his message. We still believe in power and force. We still have too much vengeance and hostility in our lives. We excuse ourselves by saying of Jesus' message, "He didn't really mean it." Well, he *showed* us he meant it, on a cross! So if we do not want to be traitors to Christ, then we dare not, we must not, miss his message of love.

Judas heard Jesus when he spoke of the Kingdom and the power and the glory. He evidently was not listening as carefully when Jesus said that the road to the kingdom of God is by way of a cross. He missed the message—and sometimes, so do we.

Judas Missed the Mandate

And sometimes, so do we. Of course, the word *mandate* means "command." The command of Jesus was to follow. The command of Jesus was to trust, to be obedient, to be faithful. This was where Judas slipped up, perhaps. Maybe he was trying to ensure success. Maybe he was trying to make Jesus do it his way. Maybe he was trying to use Jesus, trying to manipulate Jesus, trying to play God and make it all come out his way.

Don't we still do that? Don't we still try to manipulate God and use him? Think of your prayer life. What do you say in your prayers? *God do this. God do that. God bless me. God fix my problem. God give to me. God work this out for me, just like this.*

We are called to be faithful, not to be successful. We are called to serve God and to be obedient to God. We are called to do the best we know how and to trust God to bring it out right. But Judas missed the message, and he missed the mandate. And sometimes, so do we.

Judas Missed His Moment

Actually, Judas missed *two* key moments, which could have changed his life. If he had seized either of them, today his name would be an honored one rather than one of shame.

The first moment came at the Last Supper, there in the upper room. Jesus offered bread to Judas (Mark 14:17-20). This was a very significant moment. This bread was a symbol of forgiveness.

By custom, to dip a morsel of bread or meat into the dish and hand it to someone at the table was a token of deep personal friendship. Jesus was offering to Judas his love, his friendship, reconciliation, a way out of the deception—forgiveness. In effect, he was saying, "Judas, *I know*—and I still love you. It's not too late. You don't have to go through with this." The crowning blow was that even as Jesus offered this symbol of love and friendship, Judas made his final resolve to betray. Jesus saw it in his eyes; and he said to Judas, "Do quickly what you are going to do" (John 13:27b).

Still later, Judas could have been forgiven! All the disciples had run away, deserting Jesus; and yet they all were forgiven. Judas could have been forgiven, too—even after what he had done. He could have made a comeback. The big difference between Simon Peter and Judas is that while Peter failed, too, he recovered. He bounced back. But Judas thought his failure was final, and he took his own life (Matthew 27:3-5).

The unseized moments of life are the stuff tragedy is made of, the unseized moment of helping someone in need, of listening, of caring, of expressing appreciation, of giving or accepting forgiveness, of commitment.

Judas missed his moment and sometimes, so do we.

Malcolm Muggeridge is said to have written, "Both Mother Teresa and I visited Calcutta many years ago. We both saw the wretched people there and shivered. She stayed and did something about it. I went home and did nothing."

In life's great moments, what do *you* do? Judas missed the message, the mandate, and the moment; and that was his undoing. It could be our undoing, too. You see, while it is OK to grapple with this question, Why did Judas betray? the real question for us today is, Why do we?

Study / Discussion Questions

1. Share a time when someone told you their story and your new perspective made you feel differently about them. What had prevented you from seeing the person in this different light?

2. What do you think is the real truth of Judas's story?

3. How might you sometimes be like Judas? Do you misunderstand, or are you misunderstood? What causes you to fall away from Jesus at times?

4. Reflect on / discuss what sometimes causes you to miss the message Jesus has for you. List ways to become a better follower of Christ.

5. Reflect on / discuss ways in which people try to manipulate God. What is the mandate that God has given us, and what does that mean in your life?

6. Reflect on / discuss the two key moments Judas missed that could have changed his life. What can you learn from his mistakes?

Prayer

Dear God, thank you for the opportunity to come to you at any time for forgiveness and a fresh start. Help us to learn from the example of Judas and to strive to be the best Christians we can be. May we live in love toward you and toward one another. Amen.

Focus for the Week

Remember the choices Judas made and the motivations he may have had in betraying Jesus. Consider what has caused you to betray Christ in the past. Know that there is forgiveness. Seek to do the will of God this week.

Jesus and Mary Magdalene: "Easter Is a Serendipity"

SCRIPTURE: Read John 20:11-18.

D r. Brian Bauknight tells about a first-grader who started to school a few weeks late one September because his family had just moved to town. When the first-grader arrived at school the first day, his teacher was pleased. His parents had followed all the instructions. The boy had his new books, he had his lunch money, and he had a nametag on a string around his neck. The teacher looked at the nametag, and it read "Fruit Stand." She was puzzled about that name, but the school was in a multicultural neighborhood. She had seen unusual names before, such as Sunglow and Moonbeam and Peek-a-boo; so she accepted the fact that his name was Fruit Stand.

All day long, the teacher gave him his instructions: "Fruit Stand, this is your desk." "Fruit Stand, it's time for recess." "Fruit Stand, it's time for lunch." Finally, at the end of the school day, she took him out to find his school bus and introduced him to his bus driver. "Fruit Stand, this is your bus driver."

"Where do I let him off?" asked the bus driver. "I don't know," answered the teacher. "It's on the back of his nametag," said the bus driver. The teacher turned over the nametag and found the word *Anthony*!

Something like that happened to the disciples of Jesus. They did not read the signs correctly, and they did not really know who he was until the Resurrection. They did not understand. They really did not get it. The light bulb really did not turn on for them until they ran head-on into the serendipity of Easter.

Are you familiar with the word *serendipity*? Serendipity—it is the wonderful surprise of looking for one thing and somehow finding something better. Life is full of that kind of experience. Let me show you what I mean.

Christopher Columbus was earnestly searching for a new route to Asia when (as Emerson put it) he "stubbed his toe on America."

Louis Pasteur was trying to find a way to preserve wine when by chance he found the process known today as pasteurization.

Alexander Graham Bell was trying to improve the telegraph when he surprisingly stumbled onto the miracle of the telephone.

Hank Ketcham, the cartoonist, was trying to come up with an idea for a new comic strip; but he was having no luck. Nothing clicked until one evening when he came home and found his wife in tears. "Hank," she said, "our son Dennis is a menace!"[1] and the rest is history!

I know a man who several years ago missed his bus in Longview, Texas. Disgusted, he went into a nearby café to get a cup of coffee while waiting for the next bus. Suddenly and delightfully, he found the woman who would become his wife. Fifty years later, they are still happily married and still living in Longview, Texas; he never got on that bus.

Serendipity: looking for one thing and finding something better.

That is precisely what happened to Mary Magdalene on that first Easter morning, isn't it? She came to the tomb in search of a dead body but instead found a living Lord. She came to anoint the corpse of her crucified teacher but instead found a resurrected Savior. She came to mourn a death, but—surprise of surprises—she found a new life. Talk about a serendipity experience!

Mary had seen the anguish of Jesus. With her own eyes she had seen him betrayed by a close friend, deserted by his disciples, falsely accused by the authorities, nailed to a cross by the Romans, placed in a tomb by Joseph of Arimathea. Now she had come early on Easter morning to visit his grave, to care for his remains, to anoint his lifeless body with oils. But the tomb was empty!

Mary's broken heart was crushed even more. She thought someone had stolen the body of Jesus. *How cruel! How ruthless! How awful!* she thought. *They have taken away my Lord. They have robbed the grave. They have even stolen his body. Have they no respect for anything? Is nothing sacred to them?*

To confirm that all this was not a nightmare, she stooped again and stared into the tomb. His body was not there; it was definitely not there. Suddenly, someone was behind her. She turned, hoping this person could help her. In her distress, she thought it was the gardener. But then he called her name, "Mary." And she recognized him. It was Jesus! Then she had her serendipity—and we have ours!

At that moment, Mary realized the great truth that presents itself to us today on Easter morning, namely this:

> Jesus Christ lives.
> Jesus Christ has conquered death.
> There is no grave deep enough, no seal imposing enough, no guard powerful enough, no stone heavy enough to keep Christ in the grave.
> He is resurrected!
> He lives!
> He wins!

Sometimes we forget that, don't we? Today in our world, we often hear people say things like this: "Well, love is nice; but it won't work. You have to have power and clout in this tough world. And kindness is a wonderful virtue; but when crunch time comes, you'd better carry a big stick. Sure, goodness is a fine thing to strive for; but when evil rears its head, you'd better be ready to fight fire with fire." That is often what the world says to us, isn't it? "Might, force, power, intimidation—those are the things that win," the world tells us.

Then along comes Easter to remind us that, ultimately, evil does not have a ghost of a chance. Wrongdoing eventually is a dead-end street. Hate and hostility are doomed to failure because God is still God, and his truth and love cannot be defeated. God's truth and love are the most powerful things in the world; and once each year, Easter comes around to tell us that again.

Time and again, the world tries to crucify God and his love. Time and again, the world tries to crucify God and his goodness. Time and again, the world tries to crucify God and his truth. But then Easter comes and grabs us by the scruff of the neck and says, "Look! God wins! You can't kill the things of God. They will not die! They will not be vanquished! They cannot be defeated!" You may push them down for a while, but they resurrect! They rise again! They survive! They endure to the end of time.

Spires outlast spears. Altars outlast armaments. The eternal goodness of God outlasts the Golgothas of human history. This is the incredible, amazing, exciting message of Easter. On Good Friday, evil had its best chance to defeat God and could not do it. Christ conquered death! He came out of the grave! God won the victory.

Remember how powerfully Julia Ward Howe expressed it in "The Battle Hymn of the Republic":

> He has sounded forth the trumpet that shall never call
> retreat;
> he is sifting out the hearts of men before his judgment seat;
> O be swift, my soul, to answer him; be jubilant, my feet!
> Our God is marching on.[2]

That is what Easter is about. The good news is that God wins, and he wants to share that Easter victory with you and me. He wants us to join the march. He wants us to share in the triumph.

Now, with that in mind, let me bring this closer to home by suggesting three ways Easter touches our lives today.

First, Easter Is a Serendipity for Us Because It Turns Our Sorrow Into Joy

Mary came to the tomb that first Easter morning in the spirit of gloom and sadness; but there at the grave, even there, she found joy unspeakable. Strange as it may sound, so can we.

We all have to go through our dark, painful, sorrowful Good Fridays; but then on the other side of Calvary is the incredible joy of Easter morning. We all have to die, but Easter dramatically shows us that God is on both sides of the grave and that nothing—nothing, not even death—can separate us from God and his love.

Some time ago, I received a telephone call from a young woman. "Jim," she said, "we brought Mother home from the hospital this morning. She doesn't know it yet, but the report is not good. They tell us that she has six months or so to live. We want you to come and tell her."

When I arrived at her home, the mother was sitting in the den in front of a large picture window, watching her five-year-old granddaughter playing in the backyard. We chatted for a few minutes; and then she said, "Well, Jim, looks like you drew the short straw."

"What do you mean?" I asked her.

"I know that you've come to give me the bad news, haven't you? How long do I have?"

"Well, as you know, these things are uncertain," I answered; "but they are thinking six months or so."

"I'm not surprised," she said.

Then I asked her, "How do you feel inside right now?"

She answered, "Well, when I look out there and see my granddaughter, it breaks my heart to know that I won't be here to help her grow up; and I feel like crying."

I told her I felt like crying with her, and we did cry a little; but then she said, "But you know, Jim, I'm not afraid. All of my life, I've been in the church; and I believe with all my heart what you folks preach and teach—that God loves us, that God will always be there for us even when we die. So I'm ready. I'm at peace. I'm really not afraid to die."

Seven months later, she died. And when she breathed her last, her countenance was so beautifully serene. Even at the place of death, you could visibly see confidence and joy in her face. Do you know why? Because of Easter! It turns our sorrow into joy and confidence.

Second, Easter Is a Serendipity for Us Because It Turns Our Despair Into Hope

Some years ago in a small town, a baby boy was born out of wedlock. As he grew up, life was tough for him. Some children were not allowed to play with him. He was shunned on the playground. People whispered behind his back and called him ugly names. He was scarred and marked for life. He felt rejected and worthless. However, on his own, when he got to high-school age, he started going to church; but he stayed way in the background. Then one Sunday morning as he was leaving the sanctuary, he heard the minister call his name. As he stopped and turned, he heard the minister say those words he had come to dread: "Whose boy are you, anyway?"

He froze in place, felt his whole body tense up, wished that he could disappear and just vanish right through the floor. But the minister said, "Hey, I know who you are. I know whom you belong to. I can see it now. I see the family resemblance. You are a child of God. I can tell by the way you act that you are close kin to God." The boy was speechless. Then the preacher put his big hands on the boy's shoulders and said to him, "Son, you have a great heritage. Now, you go out there in the world and claim it!"

That brief incident changed that boy's life. It gave him a new identity, a new sense of worth and purpose. It turned his life around. Later, he became a great governor of one of our southern states.[3] His despair was turned to hope. The same thing happened to Mary Magdalene on that first Easter morning, and it can happen for you and me right now. Easter gives us a new heritage, a new purpose, a new identity; and it turns our sorrow into joy and our despair into hope.

Third and Finally, Easter Is a Serendipity for Us Because It Turns Our Defeats Into Victories

The cross looked like a defeat, but God made of it his greatest victory. That is the strong message of Easter: God redeems! God can take bad things and turn them into good things! God can convert defeats into victories.

A fascinating story is told about a young man barely twenty years old who was caught one day stealing sheep. He was charged and convicted. As a penalty, the villagers decided to make an example out of him. They took a branding iron and branded his forehead with the letters "ST," meaning, of course, "Sheep Thief."

The brand was permanent and was a constant source of shame to the young man. Penitent, he turned to God. He asked God for forgiveness. He asked God to help him overcome his problem. He was determined not to be remembered as a thief. With courage and with God's help, he began to live in a new way, giving to others, helping others in every way. He performed endless small acts of kindness for everyone. He was thoughtful, helpful, compassionate, caring, generous, and always dependable.

Years and years went by; and, of course, he became an old man. One day a visitor came to the village. He saw this elderly man and wondered about the letters on his forehead. He asked the people of the village what the "ST" on the man's forehead stood for. Strangely, no one could remember; but they suspected that the "ST" was an abbreviation for the word *Saint*!

Isn't that a wonderful story? And isn't that what Easter is about? Easter is a serendipity because it reminds us graphically that God, in his strength and grace, can turn

> our sorrow into joy,
> our despair into hope,
> and our defeats into victories.

Study / Discussion Questions

1. Share a time when you experienced *serendipity*, in the sense of "looking for one thing and finding something better." How did it make you feel?

2. Reread John 20:11-18. Reflect on and discuss Mary Magdalene's visit to the tomb of Jesus and talk about the different emotions she must have experienced during the course of this event.

3. In what ways does God turn sorrow into joy? What promises does God make to us regarding eternity, and how can we claim these promises?

4. During his ministry, Jesus often turned despair into hope. In what ways does God continue to turn despair into hope today?

5. Give some examples of how God turns defeats into victories. Reflect on / discuss a victory that God has given you.

6. List and discuss the meanings and messages of Easter. How has your life changed because of Easter?

Prayer

Dear God, thank you for Jesus, who died on the cross for our sins, rose from the grave, and gives us everlasting life. Help us always to keep the true meaning of Easter in our hearts. Amen.

Focus for the Week

Live in the joy and serendipity of Easter this week, that sense of expecting one thing and finding something infinitely better. Discover the victories that the resurrection of Jesus Christ makes possible. Meditate on the real message of Easter and the reality of a close relationship with God.

Notes

1. From http://www.markjuddery.com/html/tributes/2001_hank_ketchum.html

2. From "Battle Hymn of the Republic," in *The United Methodist Hymnal* (Copyright © 1989 The United Methodist Publishing House); 717.

3. Adapted from *Craddock Stories*, by Fred B. Craddock (Chalice Press, 2001); pages 156--157.